ADAM CAM'S

SAVAGE
WISDOM

This book is dedicated to my followers on Instagram and TikTok.

Your amazing energy, love, and constant support
are the reasons why I've written this book.

You're all a bunch of fucking Legends,
and I appreciate every single one of you.

FIRST THINGS FIRST...

Make no bones about it, Savage Wisdom ain't for everyone,
nor is it meant to be.

If you're averse to highly colourful language,
dark humour and the occasional spelling error...
then with all due respect, you're better off saving yourself the agro,
closing the book, and putting it back on the shelf.

Goodbye.

If that's not you, please turn the page...

WELCOME TO SAVAGE WISDOM YOU LEGEND!

My name's Adam, author of this book & preacher of Savage Wisdom.

Over the coming pages I'll take you on a journey
of self-discovery and new life perspectives.

Along the way you'll get a slap in the face, some loving hugs,
and a few tools to help make your life more enjoyable,
fulfilling and purposeful.

By the end of this book, not only will you have a firecracker under your ass,
but you'll feel ready to take on life as an empowered, spiritually aware,
badass version of yourself.

WHAT IS SAVAGE WISDOM?

In a nutshell, it's ancient wisdom, made real,
raw and relatable for the modern human.

Having been born and raised in the heart of East London,
the way I speak can be considered extremely rough around the edges,
and my style of writing follows suit.

I've written this book in the same way that I speak...
with intensity, passion, and no shortage of swear words.

Against the advice of everyone close to me,
I decided to self-publish this book,
without the aid of copywriters, ghostwriters, or even a proof-reader.

I got a "D Grade" for English GCSE's at school,
and my spelling & grammar have always been pretty shit.

So yes, there will be grammatical errors, spelling errors,
and the use of English slang within the book.

"But Adam, why would you publish a book that isn't perfectly written?"

We live in a world full of imperfect people,
expecting everything around them to be perfect.

We're told by the media, our governments, our employers
and even religion, that we need to look a certain way,
act a certain way, and speak a certain way...
regardless of if it's even true to who we are.

We're exposed to "influencers" living the perfect life,
with the perfect clothes, the perfect bodies, and the perfect skin.

Because of that, we magnify our smallest flaws
and compare ourselves to unrealistic standards.

We criticise and judge ourselves harshly for our failures,
mistakes, and fuck-ups.

None of us are perfect. None of us ever will be.

Perfection is simply an illusion that suffocates the beauty of who we are.

And it's the constant pursuit and expectance of this illusion,
that ultimately leads to so many of us living unfulfilled, empty lives.

So, if I can rebel against the norm, and self-publish my first ever book
with spelling errors, grammatical errors and English slang...

Then you can accept yourself for who you are.

You can embrace your flaws, your imperfections, your weirdness...
and be fucking unapologetic about them.

Because they are what make you the
Perfectly imperfect masterpiece you are today.

SAVAGE ART

In order to bring my powerful messages to life,
I collaborated with a young, talented illustrator named CataVic.

CataVic was able to depict my crazy, wild,
and often unconventional imagination,
into a set of truly powerful images.

Some of these images will make you laugh,
whilst others will challenge your perceptions.

The one thing they'll all do...
is inspire the fuck out of you.

CONTENTS

SAVAGE DICTIONARY

Words used in the book that you may not be familiar with, or have a different meaning than what you'd expect.

"Savage"
Something that is unapologetically real, raw & direct

"Legend"
Someone whose coolness extends beyond all space and time

"Pipe-Up"
When someone suddenly starts talking with a bit of heat, after being silent for some time

"Snowflake"
A very sensitive person.
Someone who is easily hurt, emotionally affected and/or offended by the statements of others

"Cunt"
A complete and utter asshole!
This is a gender-neutral word & has NOTHING to do with female genitalia whatsoever

"Bollocks"
A common English word used to describe a falsehood or misinformation

"Mothafucka"
A passionately aggressive way of referring to another person.
This is NOT an insult to that person

"Fuckworthy"
Something that is worth giving your time and energy to

"Absomothafuckinglutely"
A passionate way of saying "yes, of course"

"Congratumothafuckinglations"
An intensely joyous way of congratulating someone

"Tits Up"
When a situation goes extremely bad

"Unfuckwithable"
When you are truly at peace with yourself, & nothing anyone says or does
bothers you. No negativity or drama can dampen your vibe

"Flip off"
To show someone the middle finger

SLAP IN THE FACE

The wakeup call you always needed

YOU'RE GONNA DIE

...& fuck knows what happens after that.

One day, you're going to die.
And so are your best friends, your family, and everyone you care about.
Just like that. They're all going to die.

You have no real control over when it'll be, or how it'll happen.

No exceptions, and no way around it.
All you do know, is that one day... you will die.

It probably won't be pretty, like in the movies or fairy tales.
Maybe something extraordinary will happen. But probably not.

Sometimes people even have the energy to say or do
something meaningful right before they die.
And that's nice. But it's uncommon.
Most of the time, they just die.

And you're going to die too.

Some people will tell you stories about life after death,
and how beautiful it will be.
Truth is, they can't validate these stories.
Because, well... they've never died.

The only guarantee you are given after birth, is death.

You have no control over the circumstances you're born into,
nor do you have much of a say in your death.

What you do have control over,
is how you choose to experience this life you've been miraculously gifted.

So, whatever you're going through,
whether you're feeling worried, stressed or anxious...
be happy that you can even feel those things.

It means you're alive.
And while you're alive... you have options.

AGAINST ALL THE ODDS
...yet you're still here.

On your worst day...
When the world has beaten you black and blue.
When things have gone so wrong, you can hardly breathe.
When it feels as though a thousand blades are slicing into you.
When you feel like you're not good enough,
like you'll never be good enough...
Remember this:

You've already won the greatest longshot of all time.

400 QUADRILLION to 1

Those are the odds of you even existing.
Those are the odds of you reading these words right now.

Yet you still do things that make you unhappy?
You still question whether you're good enough for other people?
Or whether your life is even worth living?

You're an absolute fucking miracle.

You'd have a greater chance of playing all 180 lotteries around the world
this weekend, and winning the jackpot with each ticket.

Not only did you beat unbeatable odds...
not only did you fight to win the race to your mothers' egg...
but you've survived everything that has come your way up until now.

Those traumatic events you thought you'd never recover from...
You did.

The adversity you thought you'd never get past...
You did.

Those wounds you thought you'd never heal...
You did.

400 QUADRILLION to 1

Not only is it a miracle that you're here...
but you, yourself, have had to fight to make that miracle a reality.
It wasn't handed to you.

Deep inside of you, beyond the anxieties, stresses & fears...
is a fighter, a warrior, a survivor.
A spirit stronger than you could ever imagine.
That's who you truly are.
Don't let your friends, your family or society have you believe any different.

You my friend, are a fucking miracle.
Start living like one.

ALL THE BEAUTY
...is behind the fog.

If you woke up this morning in the comfort of a bed,
brushed your teeth, had a shower, and got dressed into clean clothes,
you're richer than 75% of people on the planet.

If you've got a bit of money in the bank and a couple of quid in your wallet,
you're among the top 8% of the world's wealthy.

And that makes it highly unlikely that you'll ever experience starvation,
like almost 25% of earth's population.

If you're in reasonably good health, you're more blessed than the
millions of people who are due to die within the next 7 days.

The fact that you're even reading this book,
means you're more educated than 95% of people in human history.

Assuming you're in the western world,
**you currently live in the freest,
most tolerable society that has ever existed.
EVER.**

You have 24/7 access to the internet,
**giving you the tools, resources, answers,
and remedies to pretty much everything in life.
The worlds library is at your fingertips!**

You are free to travel across borders by sea, air or land,
allowing you to see and experience new cultures whenever you please.

Congratumothafuckinglations... What a time to be alive!

Ok, you've heard shit like this before.
And it don't actually help much, right?

Yeah, you're lucky, and deep down you know it...
but you still struggle with your confidence, you still suffer occasional
feelings of inadequacy, and you still stress about work, money, debt,
family, friends, life... the list goes on.

ADAM CAM

Those every day struggles fog your vision and make it hard,
almost impossible to see your blessings... let alone appreciate them.

As times get harder, and more adversity comes your way,
the fog gets thicker.

This fog will leave you wandering through life unable to see the beauty
that's all around you.

So take a moment and think about the person you love most right now.
Think deeply about them and what they mean to you.
Think about how much you love that person.
Think about how they make you feel.
Think about the memories.

Now image having them taken away from you forever.
Imagine never being able to tell them you love them.
Imagine never being able to see them again.
Imagine never being able to laugh with them.
Imagine your life without them.

SOMETIMES, THE THOUGHT OF LOSING WHAT WE ALREADY HAVE,
IS THE SUN THAT CLEARS THE FOG.

DON'T BE AFRAID OF DEATH
...be afraid of living a shit life.

The ideal scenario when we die, is to have the people we love most standing around our bed, comforting us, as we peacefully pass away.

But imagine being on your deathbed...
And standing around you, as you take your final breaths...

Are the **dreams** that you never pursued.

The **ideas** you never acted on.

The **talents**, the **gifts**, and **abilities** you never used.

The **opportunities** you let slip.

The **experiences** you missed.

The **conversations** you never had.

The **love** you never expressed.

There they are, standing around your bed,
looking at you with disappointment
and sorrow in their eyes, saying...

*"We were always here for you! And you were too afraid to give us life!
& now, we'll die with you"*

And as you lay there waiting for your experience in this life to come
to an end, you begin to feel an overwhelming
sense of resentment towards yourself...
for the fear, procrastination, hesitation, and self-doubt
you allowed to hold you back.

You'd give anything just to be able to start over.

But you can't. Because you're on your deathbed...
waiting to die with the pain, shame, and self-reproach
of having let yourself down.

7

DON'T DIE HAVING NOT TRULY LIVED

Take the leap, take the risk, take the chance...
do the thing...
make the call...
take the trip...
express yourself...
forgive them...
because the pain of breaking through any amount of resistance
will never be as heart-wrenching as lying on your deathbed with regrets.

So my question is...
If you were to die today, what would die with you?

IF YOU'RE GONNA BELIEVE IN ANYTHING
...believe in your damn self.

We believe in religion, superstition, karma and psychic abilities.

We look for life's answers in astrology and star signs.

For years we even believed in the tooth fairy,
and some guy called Santa Claus, with magic reindeers.

So with all the things you believe in,
ask yourself this...

Why the fuck is it so damn hard to believe in myself?

We know the odds of winning the lottery
are over 40 million to One, but we still buy a ticket.

We know the odds of being in a plane crash
are 11 million to One, but we still board the flight.

We know the odds of being in a car crash
are 4 thousand to One, but we still get behind the wheel.

We know the odds of being attacked by a shark
are over 4 million to One, but we still swim in the sea.

So with all that being said,
and all the things you are willing to take a chance on in life,
ask yourself this...

Why the fuck is it so damn hard to take a chance on myself?

Lemme make this crystal clear for you....

The only things you haven't accomplished
are the things you counted yourself out from,
and the things you were too scared to do.

ADAM CAM

Don't let fear put your life up on a shelf,
and isolate you from being your best self.

If you need something to believe...
believe me when I tell you this...

You ARE good enough.

And yes, times get hard.
You may feel beaten, broken, and full of fear.

But no matter how many times you've been knocked down,
you're still standing right here!

Listen, you've already won the greatest battle of all time...
400 quadrillion to One

That's proof you've got ambition and drive.

So it's time for you to shift gears,
and realise...

That you're capable of achieving anything you put your mind to!

Sounds cliché as fuck, but it's true.

All you need to do...
is undo that strap use to hold yourself back,
and start believing in yourself.

Repeat loud after me...

I CAN, AND I WILL!

YOUR ACTIONS

...expose you.

You don't get in life what you pray for.
You don't get in life what you wish for.
And you don't get in life what you manifest.

Those are simply tools that'll help
to get your ass moving in the right direction.
They won't do the work for you.

You only get ever get in life what your actions are consistently aligned to.

Take a look at your life right now.
Take a good look around.
Are you happy? Are you disappointed?

Whatever you're feeling...
is the result of the actions you have taken throughout your life.

Many people say they value their health...
Yet they don't exercise regularly, eat shitty foods and don't sleep enough.

Many people say they want a loyal, trusting relationship...
Yet casually flirt with others and seek validation outside their relationship.

Many people say they want to social justice & equality...
Yet do fuck all about it other than pipe up on twitter & Facebook.

Many people say they want to be an entrepreneur...
Yet go out partying every weekend, stay up late watching Netflix,
and quit as soon as they fail.

No matter what you tell yourself or the rest of the world...
Your actions are a floodlight that expose you for who you are
and what you truly value.

LOVE THE FUCK OUT
OF YOURSELF
...and life will love you back.

Ahh "Self-love"
The buzziest of buzz words in the whole of personal development.

Run a scented bubble bath, get a manicure, have a facial,
go on a shopping spree, & have some bubbly.

NO.

Real self-love is hard.
Fucking hard.

It ain't pretty, it's not comfortable, and it doesn't feel good in the moment.
It's the hardest, yet most rewarding thing you can ever do.

Here's the side of self-love that isn't glamorised in magazines
and fancy Instagram pages...

Calling yourself out on your own bullshit and toxic behaviour,
in order to grow.

Setting boundaries & not lowering them for anyone,
because you know your worth.

Never blaming or complaining,
because you are in control of your life.

Being true to who you are in every situation,
because you are good enough.

Saying no without hesitation,
because you value your time and energy.

Staying true to your values,
because you respect yourself.

Taking care of your health,
so you can show up as your best self.

SAVAGE WISDOM

Self-love is a constant, on-going journey.
It's something that is earned day in and day out.
It's the willingness to delay instant gratification for better things to come.

When you truly love yourself, you glide through life in full flow,
appreciating everything yet needing nothing.

STATEMENTS WITH THE POWER
...to fuck your life up.

Sometimes we say things without any real consideration for the
underlying message contained within the words we have chosen to speak.

The words you choose to use are powerful.
And when spoken, plant seeds within your subconscious mind.

These seeds grow over time, shaping and distorting the way
you view yourself and the world around you.

Some statements are disguised as innocent everyday phrases.
However, said with enough repetition, they'll become a habit...
And once they're a habit, they'll become a belief.
And once they're a belief, well... you're fucked.

Here are three of those statements...

"EASIER SAID THAN DONE"

A statement that guarantees the person whose mouth it comes from,
a mediocre life at best and a meaningless existence at worse.

It's hidden meaning...

"It can be done... but I'm too lazy to do it"
"It can be done... but I'm too scared to do it"
"It can be done... but I'd prefer to settle for less coz that's what I'm used to"
"It can be done.... but I don't believe I'm worthy"

It's a statement that seems innocent enough,
yet under the surface it ruthlessly disempowers anyone
who mutters the words.

"I'll BE HAPPY WHEN..."

A statement that guarantees the person whose mouth it comes from,
will never actually be happy.

Happiness is something you experience in the now,
not in some made up reality called the future.

14

It's like a rainbow...
You can chase the mythical pot of gold, or you can stop and appreciate
the beauty right in front of you before it disappears.

"MY DESTINY IS WRITTEN IN STONE"

A statement that guarantees the person whose mouth it comes from,
a life of default rather than design.

Truly believing that your life's path has already been decided
by something or someone higher than yourself,
takes away your power of choice.

Whether it's a bad belief...
"I'm destined to be a failure"

Or even a good belief...
"It's my destiny to win!"

The underlying message you're telling yourself here,
is that you are not the one responsible for either
your failures or your successes.

This lack of responsibility for the bad in your life...
renders you powerless to make any change to your circumstance,
condemning you to a life of victimhood and blame.

While the lack of ownership for the good in your life...
disempowers and belittles who you are and what you're capable of.

YOU ARE THE SOLE ARCHITECT OF YOUR LIFE.
AND THAT MAKES YOU A POWERFUL MOTHAFUCKA.

Be conscious and stay self-aware of the words you choose to use.
They are shaping your experience in this world more than you'd imagine.

QUIT STABBING YOURSELF IN THE BACK

From your own worst enemy, to your best friend

Life, at times, will test you, challenge you, tease you,
and even push you so close to the edge that you'll end up
questioning everything.

Then, just as you feel as though things are beginning to look good,
more adversity is thrown your way...
almost as if you are being stabbed in the back by life itself.

What if I told you that life is actually on your side?
And is chomping at the bit to give you an amazing experience
during your time alive.

You see, life is constantly rolling out the red carpet infront of you,
giving you signs, opportunities and lessons to help you flourish.

The trouble is, this "red carpet" can seem as though it's laced
with pain, struggle, hardship, and adversity.

It's this perception, that can cause so many of us to believe
that life is conspiring against us.

When in reality; the challenge that life presents to us,
is the ultimate form of love... TOUGH LOVE.

Over the next few pages we'll look at the seven most common ways
in which people unwittingly stab themselves in the back...
sabotaging their own happiness and potential.

SAVAGE *WISDOM*

Enter this part of the book with an open mind,
and take it as an opportunity to sharpen your self-awareness.

Allow some time to reflect on how each self-sabotaging behaviour
could be stabbing you in the back, and how the "Savage Advice" provided
could help to heal those wounds.

Re-read this chapter at least three times, to really benefit from it.

Ready to heal up some of those self-inflicted stab wounds?

Cool, let's do it...

QUIT BATHING IN SHIT

*Having a victim's mentality is like bathing in your own shit,
then wondering why you smell*

We all bullshit ourselves in some way.
So much so, that some of us end up covered in shit.

Sometimes our bullshit is so good and so believable that not only do we buy
into it, but others do too... leaving them covered in shit as well.

This "bullshit" is a story that we tell ourselves as to why we can't
achieve or accomplish something.

Over time, with a bit of repetition, we then create an identity of ourselves
based on the story we have created in our mind.

This self-imposed identity sabotages our ability to make any change
to our life's circumstance, rendering us absolutely fucking helpless,
while we flap around in our own shit, blaming everyone and everything
for our short comings in life.

Listen to me, that's not you!

Before you ever even consider pointing your finger
at anyone or anything for your struggles, hardships or adversity,
remember this...

You may not be to blame for your current situation...
but you ARE fully responsible for how you choose to respond to it.

By accepting and owning that responsibility, you sidestep the shit bath
and instantly regain the power to control your life.

SAVAGE ADVICE

It's so easy for even the most optimistic happy-go-lucky people
to slip into moments of victimhood.

The trouble is, once you start sliding, the slope gets slipperier...
and before you know it, you've slid smack bang into the middle
of a shit bath "pity party."

To avoid the slippery slope, and subsequently covering yourself in shit...
simply switch disempowering STATEMENTS into empowering QUESTIONS.

"My boss is an asshole! I hate my job!"
What can I do to get another job?
How can I win my boss over?

"I'm so fat/skinny! My body is horrible."
Am I consistently doing what needs to be done to achieve the body I want?
What can I do to make it happen?

"My ethnicity/sexuality/gender makes it harder for me to excel!"
Are there people like me who have achieved what I want?
How did they do it? What do I need to do to follow in their footsteps?
What can I do to break the mould, and be a pioneer to inspire others
like me?

Statements close the mind, questions open it.

The sooner you start asking open questions,
instead of making disempowering statements...

the sooner you'll wash the shit off your body,
and step into the empowered life you were meant to live.

FLIP OFF THE MONKEYS

You're just a spectator

Overthinking can drag you into deep dark holes
you really don't wanna go down.

And once you're in the hole, it can be a fucking nightmare trying to get out.

You see, the thoughts in your head are like wild, rebellious monkeys
who jump around banging a drum, whilst shitting all over the place.

Pretend the monkeys ain't there...
and they'll hit you, bite you, and shit all over you to get attention.

Try to control the monkeys...
and they'll throw you head-first down the deepest,
darkest hole you can imagine.

You can't ignore or control the little fuckers...
you've just gotta change the way you engage with them.

You see, the thoughts going through your head,
are not actually your thoughts.

They are just contortions of past experiences, future assumptions,
and some random shit from your subconscious mind.

They do not define you in any way,
nor are they always an accurate reflection of what's real.

They are just a bunch of monkeys...
jumping around, making noise.

Their sole power comes from your attachment to them.
That attachment allows them to grow, manifest, and consume you.

Cutting this "attachment" tames the wild monkeys and sets you free.

SAVAGE ADVICE

The next time you feel yourself being dragged down a dark hole
by the Monkey in your mind, try this...

Close your eyes.

Imagine yourself in the front row of a theatre.

*Observe, as your thoughts enter the stage in front of you,
one by one.*

*Don't resist them, don't question them,
& don't identify yourself with them.*

*Just observe.
You are simply a spectator.*

*When a thought enters the stage that you don't like (the monkey),
Don't demonise it.*

*Simply raise your right arm,
keeping your hand closed & facing towards you...
then, with a soft smile on your face,
slowly extend your middle finger, in the monkey's direction.*

SAVAGE WISDOM

Now watch as the disheartened monkey leaves the stage
with its tail between its legs.

When a good thought enters the stage;
a thought that evokes positive emotions or empowers you...
welcome it with open arms, applaud it, cheer it, and embrace it.

Then watch on as more good thoughts begin to take the stage,
one after another.

You see, your thoughts are like clusters, travelling around your mind
attracting other thoughts of the same energetic frequency.

Whichever thought you give more attention to,
attracts more of the same.

You'll never be able to stop monkeys from getting on that stage.
But by dissociating yourself from them,
and simply observing with your middle finger held high...
they'll lose their hold over you, and give way
to more positively charged, empowering thoughts.

It's your stage, and you decide who gets the limelight.

PROTECT YOUR FUCKS

Giving a fuck about everyone and everything
will leave you fuckless real quick

It's in our DNA to give a fuck.
We are born social creatures & value the acceptance of our peers.

Our primal ancestors needed the acceptance
of their tribe in order to survive.
Without that, they would've been left behind in the wilderness,
to fend for themselves.
(Not good, with Woolly Mammoths and Sabretooth Tigers stomping about).

While the notion of being liked and accepted
has primal evolutionary roots...
it's shift from survival instinct to social necessity,
has become one of our greatest obstacles to self-acceptance.

In modern society, the addiction to what other people think,
represses us, which in turn keeps us in a sort of purgatory,
afraid of the consequences of pursuing the life we really want.

Yet, at the same time we still have this innate desire buried deep within us,
to be accepted, liked, admired, and appreciated.

We've just gotta be selective with what we give a fuck about,
rather than tossing our fucks at everyone and everything.

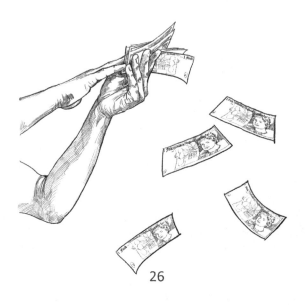

SAVAGE *WISDOM*

So with that being said,
I'd like to ask you a few questions...

Why do you give a fuck about what people think of you?
Do you even know why you give a fuck about what people think of you?

No, more than likely you don't know why you give a fuck
about what people think of you.

Because if you did know why you gave a fuck
about what people thought of you...

You probably wouldn't give a fuck about it in the first place.

Save them fucks of yours...
for something more fuckworthy.

SAVAGE ADVICE

Firstly, understand that most people are too busy dealing
with their own insecurities, traumas and personal battles to even really
notice (or give a shit) about the "thing" you're most self-conscious about.

Secondly, realise that their opinions have nothing to do with you
and everything to do with them, their past, their judgements,
their expectations, their likes, their dislikes.

Some people will hate your style,
and some will love it.

Some people will misinterpret your words and think you talk shit,
and others will love everything you have to say.

Some will hate you because you remind them of their annoying cousin,
others will feel compassionate towards you because you remind them
of someone they care about.

Each of them will get *the exact same you*. But their opinions of you will vary.
And that has *nothing* to do with you & *everything* to do with them.

No matter what you do some people will never like you.
And no matter what you do some people will always like you.

Either way, it has nothing to do with you. And it's none of your business.

So hold on tight to your bucket of fucks,
and only give them to the people & things that truly deserve them.

STOP CHATTIN' SHIT

Shit from your ass, not your mouth

Your subconscious mind is like a genie.

However, instead of granting you 3 wishes,
the genie in your mind gives you a blank canvas to tell him
what it is that you want from him.

You probably didn't realise this,
but you've been painting on this canvas since you were a kid.

Everything that you say about yourself and your life
(both in your head and out loud)
gets painted onto the canvas as your "wish".

Based on what you consistently, repetitively paint on this canvas,
the genie will give you more of.

The genie cannot distinguish between what's good or bad.

If you keep saying shit, he assumes you like it,
& want more of the same.

So, he'll grant your wish by aligning your thoughts, your feelings,
and your actions to what you have painted on the canvas.

This then creates your reality.

SAVAGE ADVICE

If there's shit all over your canvas right now, don't worry.

Every day the genie presents you with a fresh clean slate.

All you need to do is start making a conscious effort
to stop shitting from your mouth.

Remember, shit won't create your masterpiece.

The words you choose to use are a huge reason why
you're experiencing the life you live right now.

Be self-aware and pay attention to whenever you say something
negative about yourself or your life.

If you do, check yourself on it immediately, and take a moment to visually
picture yourself wiping that piece of shit off your canvas.

Then replace it with a more positive, empowering version of the statement.

Here's an example of chatting shit:
"This is too hard. I'll never be able to do this"

And here's an example of creating a masterpiece:
"Wait a minute. This may be hard, but it's not impossible."

Being self-aware enough to catch yourself in the act of chatting shit,
and strong enough to neutralise the statement, is the first step in creating
a life that you love to life.

The second step is to use the power of repetition and intensity to create a vivid masterpiece that never fades.

Every morning, as soon as your eyes open, get to work on your masterpiece.

Choose a phrase that aligns with you and how you want to feel.

A powerful example, is the phrase…

"I AM ENOUGH"

We live in a society where we're encouraged to always want more. And it's that constant chasing for more, that leave us feeling like we're not enough.

Not rich enough
Not successful enough
Not smart enough
Not attractive enough
Not slim enough

It's this lack of "enoughness" that unfortunately keeps many of us in a place of lack, no matter what we do or what we achieve.

The phrase "I am enough" said with repetition and intensity, will slowly begin to reshape the beliefs you hold about yourself and your life.

Over time you'll become grateful for all that you are and all that you have.

And when you operate from a place of abundance, abundant experiences will begin to come your way.

Feel free to adjust the phrase, or change the wording altogether, so that it resonates with you on a deeper, more personal level.

Repeat your chosen phrase over and over…
While you're prepping your breakfast, brushing your teeth, in the shower, or even on the way to work.

Say it loud, or say it in your head…
it don't matter, just get it on the canvas.

The more you do this, the more of a masterpiece you'll begin to create.

Said with repetition and intensity,
this'll begin to rewire your subconscious mind,
by aligning your thoughts, feelings and actions
to the words you are speaking.

As the phrase becomes natural to you, start saying it with a bit of oomph.
Attach some fucking passion to it.

Say it loud, say it proud.

Look yourself in the mirror, make eye contact,
and say your phrase with confidence, certainty & intent.

KILL THE MOTHAFUCKA YOU'VE CREATED
Wearing a mask suffocates your authenticity

We're born into this world as a tiny, vulnerable human being,
without a single preconceived notion of our identity.

At birth we have no idea who we are, what we are...
or what the fuck is going on around us.

There's no façade, no persona and no ego.

It don't matter who we're with, or who's around us.
We cry till we're fed, and shit when we feel like it.

We are in essence, the purest form of authenticity.

As we mature through the early stages of life,
we begin to create a character based on the environment
and people we are exposed to.

Family values, cultural norms and the "rules of society"
are thrust upon us like a tonne of bricks,
and we're expected to conform, regardless of how we actually feel.

To cope with the weight of this expectation,
along with the subconscious need to "fit in" and be accepted...
a new artificial identity is formed.

This new identity suppresses who we really are
and suffocates our authenticity...
leading us to live an unfulfilling, disempowered life.

This perception of who we are, dictates our current thoughts,
feelings, and subsequent actions.

And it's those "actions" that create the life
we're experiencing right now.

In a nutshell, your life at present is nothing more
than accumulated past conditioning.

So, you are not who you are today as a result of your past,
but because of your past.

The beauty of that...
is that you're living in your future's past right now.

SAVAGE ADVICE

Picking and choosing when to be the "real" you,
fundamentally fucks your life in two ways.

Firstly, being a social chameleon slowly eats away at your self-worth...
like a maggot eating its way through a dead corpse.

Every time you change the way you speak, dress, walk or behave,
to suit the environment around you...
you subtly tell yourself that the "real" you ain't good enough.
This reinforces the character that society
has created for you throughout your life...
whilst further suffocating and disempowering your authentic self.

SAVAGE WISDOM

Secondly, as the old saying goes...
"Your vibe attracts your tribe"

So, if you're not living true to who you are in every situation,
you'll inevitably attract people into your life
who vibe with the fake persona you're presenting, NOT the real you.

Over time this becomes a heavy burden, and closes the door to what could
be some amazing connections that set your heart and soul on fire.

Instead, the door remains wide open to people you don't really vibe with.
And that right there, is the recipe for a miserable, unfulfilling, empty life.

Listen, showing up every day as your truest, realest self ain't easy.
Far from it actually.

The fear of exposing the REAL you to the world can be daunting.

Yes, you will lose some friends.
Yes, you will piss some people off.
Yes, you will question whether you're doing the right thing.

The road to authenticity can be a very lonely path to begin with.
But rest assured, continuing on that path will lead you to a much
happier life.

Be real, be you, and be fucking unapologetic about it.

LOOK FOR THE GOLDEN NEEDLE

Stop looking for shit & you might stop seeing it

As a human on planet Earth,
you're naturally hardwired to be a negatively charged, pessimistic cunt...
or at least, massively prone to being one.

Our innate tendency to emphasise and focus more attention
on the negative, is a result of our evolution as a species.

It's why negative news gets reported and spread so much more readily.
It's why we can't turn away from a car accident or two people fighting.
It's why it's so much more tempting to relate to others through complaining
and gossip rather than through gratitude.
It's just easier.

Earlier in human history, paying close attention to bad, dangerous,
and negative threats in the world was literally a matter of life and death.

Those who were more attuned to danger and who paid more attention to
the bad things around them were more likely to survive.

So, to help us survive during our time on Earth,
our neanderthal ancestors passed onto us a gift...
a pair of invisible glasses.

Over the centuries these glasses have helped our ancestors survive by
allowing them to spot the bad and the dangerous in every situation.

As the centuries have passed by, so have the dangers of prehistoric living...
like being eaten alive by wild animals, and treacherously
travelling through snow, sleet, and ice.

With a completely different world around us, and evolution not having fully
caught up just yet, we are all still born into this world with the same
prehistoric glasses gifted to us by our ancestors.

These glasses show us the world with a pessimistic lens.
They magnify the bad in every situation.
They cause us to dwell on mistakes, failures, and fuckups.
They highlight our flaws, insecurities,
and the things we hate most about ourselves.

36

So, as well as keeping our species alive and thriving,
these glasses also keep many of us in a constant state irritation and stress...
which hinders us from experiencing a truly fulfilling life in modern society.

Unless you're consciously aware of these glasses,
they'll blind you from seeing just how fucking magnificent you,
and the world around you really are.

SAVAGE ADVICE

Removing the glasses placed upon you at birth,
will open your field of vision to a brand-new perspective on life.

It'll allow you to experience your time on earth with joy, fulfilment,
and a whole load of happiness.

Is it easy to remove the glasses from your face? Fuck no.

If it was, everyone would be skipping along farting fairy dust
& magical rainbows, whilst living on cloud nine.

And as you know, that ain't the case.

Removing the glasses is a gradual process,
that requires a bit of consistency, persistence, and self-awareness.

Then once they're off, you can chuck 'em to the floor,
step on 'em a few times and enjoy your new reality.

Sound good?
Cool, here's how you do it...

No matter how bad of a shit storm you find yourself in,
immediately shift your focus to finding a "golden needle"

The golden needle is essentially the ONE positive thing
you can take away from what is happening.

Now listen, finding a golden needle in a big pile of shit,
whilst in the midst of a shit storm... ain't easy.

Most people will say "fuck this shit!" (no pun intended),
and simply retreat to the nearest shelter, then watch the shit storm unfold
from a distance whilst complaining about how bad it is.

Doing this makes you a living, breathing beacon for shit storms.
Essentially making you, and your entire life, a magnet for shit.

As the old saying goes...
"Where your attention goes, energy flows"
So yeah, focus on the shit, and you'll simply attract more shit.
That ain't you. You're wiser than that.

You're out there rummaging through the shit for that damn needle.
You're fucking relentless in your pursuit to find that little fucker,
no matter what it takes.

And when you do find it (which you ALWAYS will)...
you embrace the moment, and focus all your attention on it.

What you'll then find is that you begin to see more and more
golden needles popping up all around you.

And as you give more of your attention to those needles,

the shit storm will subside, and the sun will begin to shine.

Remember, find that ONE positive from your bad situation,
and focus all your attention on it, be grateful for it,
and show massive appreciation towards it.

Making this a conscious habit, will gradually allow you to see opportunities
where others see difficulty, and solutions where most
only ever see problems.

This is your natural vision, and how you are designed to see the world.

Reclaim it!

And start experiencing this life in all its glory.

ILLUSIONS CAN'T HURT YOU

Consistently looking back fucks with your neck

Your painful experiences are nothing but illusions. They're not real.

The past is only a collection of memories.
We can't experience the past. We can only remember it.

So that "thing"...
You know, the thing that caused you pain and trauma at the time,
and is still beating you down and holding you back today...
Yeah that thing....

What if it's only real today in your mind because you keep thinking about it,
you keep retelling the story and activating the frequency
of pain associated with that memory?

Because that's all it is... a collection of memories stored in your mind,
that you choose to keep refreshing and reliving in the present moment.

The pain you feel as a result of that "thing" isn't actually tangible.
It's not happening to you in the moment.
It's only happening because of your persistent retelling of the story.

When the past happened, it wasn't the past, it was NOW.
When the future happens, it won't be the future, it will be the NOW.

All you have, and all that you'll ever have, is the NOW.

Wanna know the best part about there only ever being a now?

You have full control over it.

SAVAGE ADVICE

There's always a choice in how to respond to the illusion of past pain.

To detach from the momentum of suffering,
you've gotta direct attention inward, not backward.
Your brain then takes note, and cc's the rest of your body to get on the
same page.

Give this a go...

Sit down comfortably.

Take three deep breaths.

Look up at the sky, look outside,
and get connected with the only reality there is.
The present.

Put your hand on your chest, feel your heart.
Feel the gravity on your body.

In becoming present, perhaps you can begin to entertain a new thought...

Look for an excuse to feel good..
Any excuse.

Find aspects of your life right now that are actually doing ok.
Give them attention.

Think how they these positive aspects of your life make you feel.
Go deep down the golden rabbit hole, and allow these thoughts to
cling onto each other, growing in size weight and prominence.

ADAM CAM

If a Monkey enters your thoughts (which it no doubt will),
you know what to do.

From that place, you'll find yourself exiting the mental rat race, the hustle,
the struggle & the suffering...

Maintain this new trajectory and you'll begin to see new scenery...
you'll start thinking different thoughts, feeling new feelings...

and before you know it,
you've guided yourself into an entirely new eco-system.

An eco-system where you start feeling good for no reason...
other than because you can.

And then you look back at the suffering, and realise...
"WOW I really worked hard at maintaining that!
I could've walked away at any time!"

Once you begin to shift your focus into the present moment,
you detach from the momentum of illusionary suffering, aka the past.

50
SAVAGE REMINDERS

Powerful reminders you need for life

WHEN LIFE THROWS YOU IN THE MIDDLE OF A SHIT STORM...

BREATHE, AND REMEMBER WHO THE FUCK YOU ARE.

Life will test you.
Life will challenge you.
Life will push you to the edge.
And life will make you cry.

When it does...
Remember who lives in the place
beyond your anxieties, stresses, worries and fears.

Yeah, that mothafucka is a badass.

And that badass has overcome everything life has
thrown their way.

Don't you ever forget it.

TOXIC
POSITIVITY

CORRODES
THE SOUL

Some days you'll feel like shit...
where fear, anger and sadness consume you.

That's cool. You're human.
You're not Mary Poppins.

Attempting to avoid, silence, or cover up
these negative emotions will allow them to
take up residence inside of you...
where they'll grow, manifest,
and eventually cling-on to your vibe.

Accept your negative emotions,
observe them and reflect on what you're feeling.

Then you can decide on the best action
for your healing.

Remember...
If you keep sweeping your feelings under the rug,
you'll eventually trip from all the mess you've made.

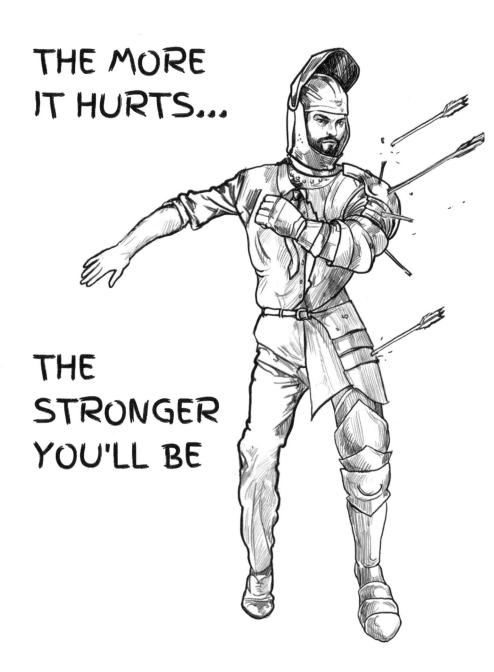

THE MORE
IT HURTS...

THE
STRONGER
YOU'LL BE

You don't build emotional strength
or psychological resilience,
by having everything go your way 100% of the time.

You build them by getting better at dealing
with adversity when it comes your way.

It won't feel like it at the time, but every rejection
every failure and every heartbreak that you experience,
adds another piece of metal to your armour.

Not only to strengthen you...
but to give you the wisdom, that'll one day,
help & inspire the people you love most,
when they need you most.

Next time a situation comes to hurt you,
don't curse the sky. Praise it.

Because it's carving you into the absolute
fucking Legend you are destined to be.

LEARN TO LOVE THE SOUND OF YOUR OWN FEET WALKING AWAY

FROM MOTHAFUCKAS WHO ARE NO GOOD FOR YOUR HEAD, YOUR HEART & YOUR SOUL.

The more you walk away from things
that clutter your head, hurt your heart,
and drain your vibe...

The healthier & and happier your life will be.

Value yourself enough to walk away.

BEFORE YOU TRY
"FIXING" OR "HEALING"
SOMEONE ELSE...

MAKE SURE
YOU AIN'T
DAMAGING OR WOUNDING
YOURSELF IN THE PROCESS.

Not prioritising YOUR energy,
is the ultimate disservice to everyone you care about.

Your family, friends and the people you love,
deserve the best version of you...

The YOU who is full of life, light,
energy and vibrance.

So when you notice your vibe
deteriorating around a certain person...
get the fuck outta there as quickly
& compassionately as you can.

Your energy is a priority.
Protect the shit out of it.

YOUR TOLERANCE TEACHES PEOPLE HOW TO TREAT YOU

Stop asking yourself...
"Why is this happening to me?"

And start asking yourself...
"Why the fuck am I allowing it!?"

People learn how to treat you based on
what you continuously accept from them.

These mothafuckas know your worth.
They're just hoping that you don't.

Remember...
What you condone, sets the tone.
Always.

AVOID MOTHAFUCKAS WHO KEEP PUSHING YOU OVER THE EDGE...

THEN ASKING HOW YOU FELL OFF

Some people will do everything they can to push your
buttons and provoke a reaction from you...
then play "victim" once they succeed.

If a particular person has a habit
of trying to get under your skin...
start making it a habit of yours
to call them out on it instantly.

They'll say shit like:

"Oh, you've got it all wrong"
or
"Oh, you're being so insecure"

Fuck what they say.

Don't play their game.
Stand by your words and set your boundaries.

And if they disrespect you again,
value yourself enough to burn the damn bridge.

GUT FEELINGS GOT YOUR BACK

FOLLOW YOUR HEART...
**It will take you to places that
ignite the fire within your soul.**

WHILST...

LISTENING TO YOUR HEAD....
It's the voice of reason.

AND...

ALWAYS TRUSTING YOUR GUT.
It's your Guardian Angel.

ALLOWING A TOXIC PERSON BACK INTO YOUR LIFE...

IS LIKE REHEATING KFC & THINKING IT'LL STILL BE FINGER LICKIN' GOOD.

You don't ever have to feel guilty about removing
toxic people from your life completely.

If their presence costs you your peace of mind,
robs you of your happiness,
or drains your soul...

They gotta go.

Life's too short and way too fucking valuable
to be wasted with people who you aren't aligned with.

THEY'RE ALWAYS GONNA HAVE SOMETHIN' TO SAY...

BAD NEWS:
You can't make people like, love, understand, validate, accept or be nice to you.

GOOD NEWS:
It doesn't fucking matter.

Wanna know what really matters?

Liking, loving, understanding, validating, accepting and being nice to YOURSELF.

STOP TRYNA
JUSTIFY YOURSELF

Every time you over explain yourself...
what's really happening is you trying to make the
situation less awkward, either for them or for you.

When you continuously justify,
your self-worth depletes just a little bit more every time.
And by doing so, you give away your power.

So...
Say what you need to say.
Say it with certainty.
Say it with conviction.

Then walk away, and step back into your power.

GETTIN' A TEXT BACK
DON'T VALIDATE YOUR EXISTENCE...

IF THEY GHOST YOU,
RESPECT THE DEAD
& MOVE THE FUCK ON

Someone disappearing on you
doesn't reflect on your worth.

It reflects their insecurities and emotional immaturity.

Thank 'em for the free trial...
then say goodbye with your middle finger held high.

STOP SAYING "YES" AND "OK"

TO THE PEOPLE YOU SHOULD BE SAYING "NO" AND "FUCK OFF" TO

Stop giving a fuck about losing people.

Start giving more fucks about losing yourself
by trying to please everyone.

Saying NO is pretty fucking amazing once you learn
how to say it unapologetically.

Saying NO will save you time, energy,
peace of mind and heartache.

Say NO to make it clear where you stand.

Say NO to people who overstep their boundaries
and make unfair demands.

If they still don't get it, Remember...

You can have a good heart, a kind nature,
and a loving soul, yet still tell people
to FUCK OFF when needed.

DON'T TRUST WORDS...

MOST PEOPLE TALK SHIT

Most people tend to shit more from their mouth, than they do from their ass.

Don't trust what they tell you.

Trust what they show you on a consistent basis.

Actions and patterns don't lie.

IF THEY KEEP DISRESPECTING YOUR BOUNDARIES...

BURN THE FUCKING BRIDGE

If standing up for yourself means
that you burn the bridge...

Go grab the gasoline, grab a match,
and set that mothafucka alight!

Cutting off people who consistently disrespect you
and your boundaries, is one of the greatest acts of love
that you can show to yourself.

And if they're family, remember...
Blood ain't thicker than peace.

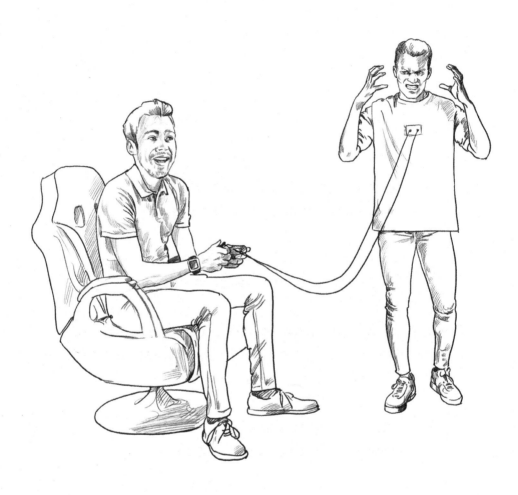

STOP GIVING PEOPLE
THE POWER TO PLAY YOU

If you try to "control" your emotions,
they'll make you a slave...
allowing the person whose triggering you,
to be your master.

The more you try to stop being pissed off,
the angrier you'll get.

The more you try to stop being stressed,
the more you'll freak the fuck out.

You cannot control your emotions.
Let them be.

Feel them, embrace them,
and let them flow through you.

Focus your energy on your reactions and behaviours
in response to feeling those emotions.

Learn to separate your emotions from your actions,
and you'll be no one's slave.

THEIR
MIXED
SIGNALS
MEAN NO...

GET
THE FUCK
OUTTA
THERE

Deciphering mixed signals, along with the overthinking
that comes with them, can be draining as fuck.

Your time & energy are too valuable
to try and work that shit out.

So, instead of allowing them to leave you feeling
confused, frustrated and unsure...
be straight up, and communicate firmly.

If the signals are still leading to nowhere,
show yourself the respect you deserve...

AND GET THE FUCK OUTTA THERE.

THE PERPETUAL ABILITY TO START OVER...

IS YOUR SUPERPOWER

If you don't like your friends...
go make new friends.

If you're in a miserable relationship...
communicate, or break the fuck up.

If you hate your job...
start looking for a new job, or learn new skills.

If you don't like being told what to do...
start your own business and be your own boss.

You are under absolutely no obligation to keep
repeating toxic, miserable cycles in your life.

Yes, it's "easier said than done"
to just start from scratch...

but whether you like to admit it or not,
the choice is always yours.

And having the ability to choose,
makes you the architect of your own life.

CONSTANTLY WORRYING ABOUT THE FUTURE...

WILL CRIPPLE YOU IN THE PRESENT

You wanna know something funny?

Most of the shit you stay up late at night
worrying about...

ain't even gonna fucking happen.

WHEN LIFE
RATTLES YOU...

WHATEVER'S
INSIDE WILL
SPILL OUT

Holding onto negative emotions without expressing,
owning, or acknowledging how they make you feel...
allows them to pour into your cup.

The longer you avoid or ignore these emotions,
the more they'll keep pouring.

Then, when things in your life go tits up
(which will inevitably happen),
everything in your cup will spill out
for the world to see, hear and feel.

Now ask yourself...
"What's inside my cup?"
"What spills out when I get shaken by life?"

Is it calmness & composure?
Or is it harsh words & aggressive actions?

Be conscious & stay aware of the emotions you are
harbouring inside of you.

It's easy to fake it, until life shakes the shit out of you.

IF YOU DON'T WANNA BE HURT BY HATE...

STOP BEING A SLAVE TO PRAISE.

If your eyes light up from their acceptance...
your heart will break from their rejection.

That makes you a slave to praise.

The truth is, in this modern world you'll never truly stop
seeking some sort of validation from others.

It's impossible.

Instead, aim to seek validation for better reasons
and from better people.

IF SOCIAL MEDIA IS THE COCAINE OF THE INTERNET...

MAKE SURE YOU'RE TAKING THE GOOD STUFF

Immediately gratifying and hugely addictive.

We want it, we crave it, and we go into withdrawal
when we're without it.

Social media is a drug that you'll most likely
continue to use for the rest of your life...

So you're better off going for the 'Grade A' Colombian
gear, rather than the shit stuff cut from rat poison.

Be conscious and purposeful with who you
choose to follow on social media.

Do they inspire you?
Do they bring light to your life?

Or do they leave you feeling
like you're not good enough?

THE MORE YOU BEG, THE MORE YOU CHASE...

THE FASTER THEY'LL RUN

Massively increase the chances of getting whatever you want in life, by cultivating the feelings associated with
ALREADY HAVING IT.

Wanna a find a romantic partner?
Cultivate a feeling of love,
by loving & accepting yourself.

Want more money?
Cultivate a feeling of abundance,
by showing deep appreciation
for everything you already have.

Cultivate the feelings first,
and you'll naturally begin to take actions
that align with getting the "thing" you most desire.

Otherwise, you'll chase it like a desperate,
needy, headless chicken...
and it'll run away from you.

IF THEY BREAK YOUR HEART
BLOW THEIR FUCKING MIND

Be everything they thought you couldn't be,
and love yourself the way you wish they did.

It's your greatest opportunity to become the Legend
you know you are capable of being.

But do it for YOURSELF before anybody else.

Be your own damn upgrade.

EXPECTING OTHER PEOPLE TO MAKE YOU HAPPY...

IS FUCKING SELFISH.

"Be with someone who makes you happy"

Bollocks!
Happiness is your responsibility.

Don't put that kind of pressure on someone else...
and don't allow someone else to have that kind of power
over how you feel on a daily basis.

Healthy, fulfilling relationships are about contributing
to each other's happiness, without any expectations.

The happiness you share with a partner
should only ever be the icing on the cake...
not the whole cake.

If you cannot find happiness on your own,
you'll place a huge burden on every
relationship you enter.

Expecting someone to provide you with happiness,
when you can't even do it for yourself,
is not only selfish... but it'll also strip you of your power,
and leave you in a constant state of neediness and lack.

Be willing to do the inner work required,
rather than weighing someone else down
with the expectation of doing it for you.

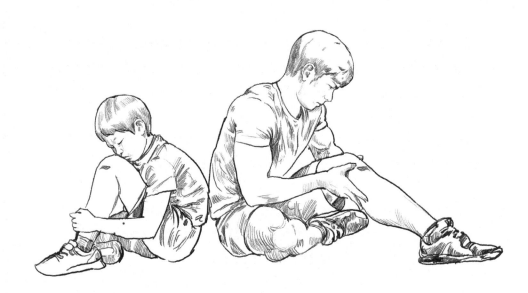

UNHEALED WOUNDS WILL KEEP BLEEDING

If you live with the mentality that...

"My trauma fucked me up!
That's why I am the way I am!"

...instead of learning to heal and grow from your trauma.
Then you are your own problem.

What happened to you as a child, is not your fault.

Being self-aware and learning to heal those
wounds as an adult, is always your responsibility.

ACT LIKE A DAMN
DOOR MAT...

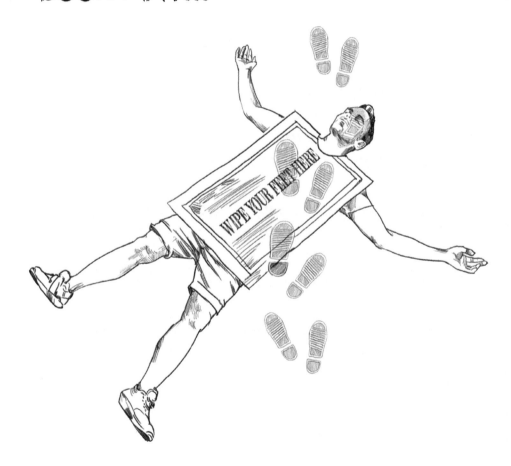

AND YOU CAN EXPECT
TO BE TREATED LIKE ONE

Everything that you tolerate...
Everything that you allow...
And everything that you accept in life...

is because you subconsciously believe
that you deserve it.

The people in your life simply mirror back
your personal belief systems.

Trauma, unhealed wounds and bad experiences
all play a role in these beliefs...
and it's up to you to do the inner work
to uncover these wounds & heal them.

If not, you'll keep scratching your head,
wondering why people continuously treat you like shit.

The realisation that you are the one
calling the shots in your life right now,
is the first big step to making a change.

Let that realisation empower you,
rather than trigger you.

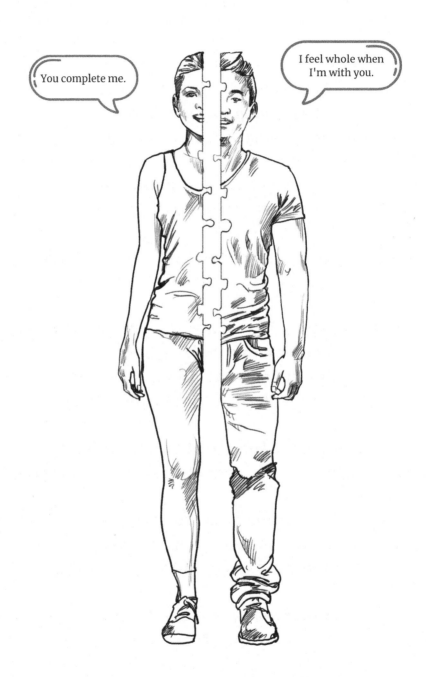

YOU AIN'T A FUCKING FRACTION

If you ever refer to your partner as...
"My other half" or worse "My better half"

I'd like to take this opportunity to remind you
that you are not a fucking fraction.

By speaking of yourself as "incomplete" you plant
subconscious seeds in your mind that reinforce
a false belief that you cannot FEEL or BE
at your best without another person.

This belief will make you lower your standards,
and tolerate things you know you shouldn't...
all for the reward of feeling whole.

Take this as a strong reminder...

YOU ARE A FULL MASTERPIECE ALL BY YOURSELF
& YOU DON'T NEED ANYONE OR ANYTHING
TO COMPLETE YOU.

MOTIVATION IS A DRUG

The need for motivation is like a junkie's
need for their next hit.

You get the hit...
you feel on top of the world...
then you crash like a mothafucka!

And the cycle repeats itself.

The constant need to be motivated
creates an energy of lack and scarcity around you...
ultimately forcing you to step out of your power
and into a lesser version of yourself.

The "motivation" you're craving is already inside of you...
you've just gotta amplify it by focusing
your spare time on the things that truly
set your heart on fire - whatever that may be for you.

The feelings cultivated from doing that consistently,
will transcend into every area of your life...
relighting that fire in your belly,
& allowing you to step back into your power.

IGNORING THE EARLY WARNING SIGNS

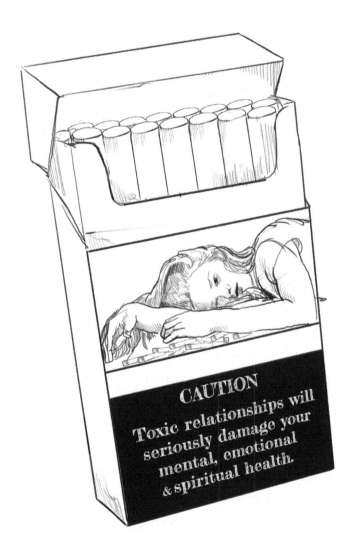

CAUTION

Toxic relationships will seriously damage your mental, emotional & spiritual health.

WILL FUCK YOU LATER DOWN THE LINE

Turning a blind eye to those red flags
will always bite you in the ass.

If you don't address and communicate your concerns in
the beginning, you'll be left with heart ache in the end.

KEEP YOUR EYES OPEN WIDER THAN YOUR HEART.

And always trust your gut.

DON'T LET THEIR DEMONS
DIM YOUR LIGHT

Living life powerfully, as your truest,
realest, most authentic self...
is the most liberating feeling any human
can experience during their time alive.

As amazing as this is...
it ain't easy.

People have a tendency to expect others
to fit inside their box of expectations.

Refusal to do so, will result in their
demons becoming irritated.

These "demons" form as a result of the pain caused
by suppressing their own authenticity.

You see, people who cannot express who they truly are,
find it difficult to accept other people living authentically.

It's something they want,
It's something they crave,
but it's something they're too afraid to do.

Don't ever let your authenticity become shrouded
by other people's expectations of you...
and likewise, always allow other people
to express who they truly are.

A world where people are free to shine their light,
is a happier world for everyone.

WHEN YOU'RE
STARVING
FOR LOVE...

THE BREADCRUMBS OF ATTENTION
THEY PRESENT TO YOU
WILL LOOK TASTY

When you're in need of love,
you're more likely to lower your standards
and boundaries in order to receive it.

That "need" will cause you to ignore red flags,
tolerate unacceptable behaviour,
and make-do with less than you deserve.

Don't settle for the damn breadcrumbs
when there's someone out there willing
to give you the entire bakery.

WORDS OF HATE
FROM THEIR MOUTH

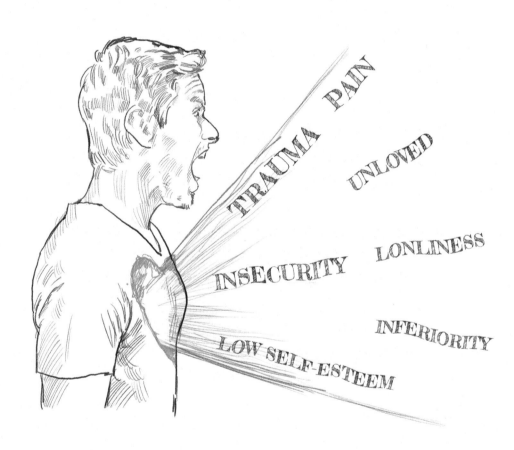

ARE A PROJECTION OF PAIN
FROM THEIR HEART

The cruel words they yell at you.
The names they call you.
The hating.
The trolling.
The bullying.

That shit has nothing to do with you,
and everything to do with them.

They have deep, unhealed, open wounds,
and are projecting their pain, struggle, trauma
and insecurities onto you.

Don't let their words weigh you down
with anger or resentment.

Instead, flip the script...
Feel sorry for them, and empathise
with their pain & suffering.

By showing compassion towards them,
you lift off the weight they have tried
to place on your shoulders,
and you give it back to them.

Showing empathy and compassion
to your haters, makes you...
UNFUCKWITHABLE.

MUZZLE YOUR EGO WHEN IT STARTS TO GROWL

The ego can be your best friend...
driving you through life with purpose, certainty,
and a fire in your belly.

It can also be your worst enemy...
making you an arrogant cunt.

An untamed ego will destroy relationships,
ruin friendships, close doors to amazing opportunities,
and limit your growth as a human being.

Love the fuck out of yourself...
but never look down at anyone.

Stand up strongly for what you believe in...
but have an open mind & show empathy.

Give honest feedback and advice...
but never belittle or judge.

Be supremely confident in who you are...
but show comfort in being vulnerable.

Make your wellbeing a number one priority...
but never neglect those closest to you.

Keeping your ego as close to the edge as you can,
without ever letting it slip off, is a one way ticket
to a highly empowered, fulfilled life.

LIFE WILL KEEP
PRESENTING YOU
WITH THE SAME
PERSON IN
DIFFERENT BODIES...

UNTIL YOU WAKE UP & START
PAYING ATTENTION TO THE LESSON
THEY'VE BEEN SENT TO TEACH YOU

The truth is, when it comes to intimacy,
we attract what we think we deserve,
what we know, and what we're used to.

No one willingly attracts the cheater, the abuser,
or the emotionally unavailable person...

but if it keeps happening, relationship after relationship,
then it's on you to take ownership and
break the toxic pattern.

Set your boundaries...
and allow no mothafucka to cross them.

Pay attention to red flags...
& address them instantly.

Do the inner work...
start learning to love, appreciate & accept yourself.

There's a toxic pattern that's begging
to be exposed & ejected.

It's up to you to wake the fuck up & get it done.

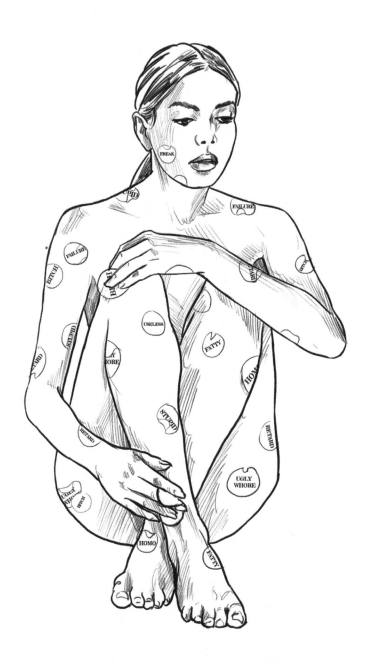

THE LABELS YOU'VE BEEN GIVEN DON'T HAVE TO STICK.

People will always label you,
judge you, and call you names...
whether you like it or not.

You can't control what other people say or do,
but you have full control over
your perspective and response.

Let 'em call you whatever the fuck they like.

As long as you know who you are, you know your worth,
and you stay 100% true to your authenticity...
those labels won't stick for long.

The power is always with you.
Claim it.

IF YOU DON'T GET IT OFF YOUR CHEST...

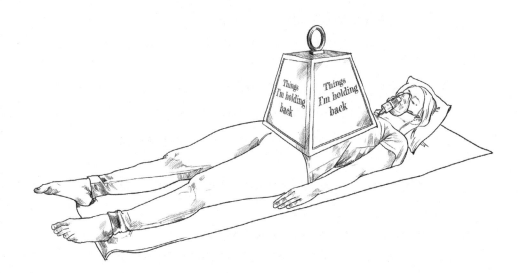

YOU'LL ALWAYS STRUGGLE TO BREATHE

If you don't communicate boundaries,
they'll always take advantage.

If you don't express your anger,
they'll keep provoking you.

If you don't communicate your needs,
they'll never be met.

If you don't express your love,
they'll assume you don't care.

If you don't communicate your thoughts,
they won't be able to read your mind.

If you don't express your feelings,
you'll suffocate who you truly are.

A lack of expression and communication will really
fuck up a lot of good things in your life.

Get it off your chest.

IF YOU CONSISTENTLY COMPLAIN WITHOUT DOING ANYTHING ABOUT IT...

LIFE WILL ALWAYS FUCK YOU HARDER

Having people feel sorry for you at your "pity party"
will not change or help your situation in the slightest.

In fact, it'll reinforce a helpless, hopeless,
victim mentality within you, that will encourage life to
FUCK YOU HARDER while you're down.

Actively, relentlessly finding solutions to your problems
& woes, is what will allow you to step out of victimhood
and into your power.

You'll be amazed at how well life starts treating you
when you take this approach.

YOU ARE THE ARTIST OF YOUR LIFE...

DON'T GIVE THAT DAMN PAINTBRUSH TO ANYONE ELSE

Whatever you are not changing in your life,
you are choosing.

I'll write that again in capitals in case you missed it...

WHATEVER YOU ARE NOT CHANGING IN YOUR LIFE,
YOU ARE CHOOSING TO BE A PART OF YOUR LIFE.

You're in control.

Not destiny.
Not fate.
Not your family.
Not your friends.
Not your boss.

YOU.

You are the artist of your life,
so don't give that damn paintbrush to anyone else.

ALLOWING YOURSELF TO BE OFFENDED...

IS LIKE VOLUNTARILY STEPPING IN DOG SHIT

Being offended is like seeing a big pile
of dog shit in the distance.

You keep your eyes fixated on it, you walk right up to it...

THEN YOU STEP IN IT

And immediately wonder why there's shit
all over your shoes.

You had the option to adjust your path & avoid the shit,
but you chose to walk straight into it.

Now you've gotta deal with the smell,
& inconvenience of having shit all over your shoes
for the rest of the day.

Feeling triggered isn't always something we can control...
but how we respond to the trigger is
completely our choice.

You can acknowledge it, then walk around it.

Or...

You can step right into it and then deal with the bad vibe
it brings to the rest of your day.

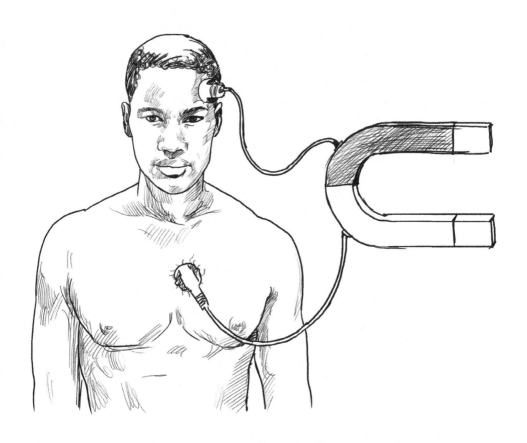

YOU ATTRACT
WHAT YOU BELIEVE
YOU DESERVE

"Life kicks you when you're down"
because when you feel like shit, you act like shit,
so you inevitably attract more shit.

"The rich get richer, the poor get poorer"
because the rich think abundant thoughts,
feel abundant feelings,
and take abundant actions.
Therefore they attract abundance.

"Positive energy attracts positive energy"
Someone who regularly thinks positive thoughts,
will feel positive feelings,
leading to them take positive actions,
which in turn, gives them a much greater chance
of attracting positive experiences into their life.

Simply put...
The thoughts you think create the feelings you feel...
the feelings you feel, fuel the actions you take...
and the actions you take, create your reality.

Bosh!

You my friend, are a living breathing magnet.

THE PERSON RESPONSIBLE FOR YOUR FUCKED UP RELATIONSHIPS...

IS...

If you've experienced numerous heartbreaks
and toxic relationships, it's important to remember
that the only constant in all of those relationships
is yourself.

So, if all of your relationships suck, or are fucking up...
then maybe you should start with the one thing
they all have in common.

Ouch.

But unequivocally true.

EMOTIONAL VAMPIRES WILL DRAIN YOU DRY

Sometimes you work with them...
Sometimes you socialise with them...
Sometimes you even live with them...

Emotional vampires are everywhere,
and prey on their unsuspecting victims
at any given opportunity.

They always seem to have problems
and dramas of some sort.

Every conversation always seems to revert
back to them & their life.
They are always the victim,
and play host to regular pity parties.

These vampires will suck the life out of you,
if you leave yourself vulnerable to their bite.

Here's how you protect yourself...

Only ever entertain conversations around
SOLUTIONS rather than PROBLEMS.

Hit them with positive "WHAT IF's..."
to counter their negative "YEAH BUT's..."

By constantly being the light to their darkness
you'll either help them change their ways,
or you'll irritate them so much they'll
avoid you at all costs. Either way, you win.

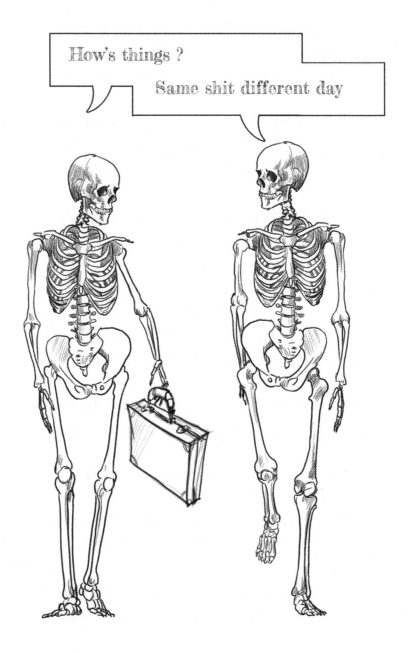

LIFE WITHOUT PASSION
IS LIKE DEATH ON EARTH.

Sex with no passion, is boring.

Kissing with no passion, is dull.

A conversation with no passion, is uninspiring.

A career with no passion, is draining.

A life with no passion, is fucking soul destroying.

Life is best lived with PASSION.

But you can't force passion onto something
you just ain't passionate about...

So, identify the things that really,
truly set your heart on fire,
and do more of that shit.

TO GET THAT
SOUL LIFTING, SPINE TINGLING,
MAGICAL KINDA LOVE WITH THEM.....
YOU GOTTA GIVE IT TO YOURSELF FIRST

The greatest gift you can give to your partner
is to love yourself.

Loving yourself makes you less needy and insecure...
allowing them space to breathe, and experience
their own self love journey.

Loving yourself makes you the master
of your own happiness...
taking the heavy burden away from them.

Loving yourself makes you more confident & assertive...
by empowering you to set boundaries,
which lead to more respect and less problems.

Loving yourself allows you to flourish and grow...
by putting your physical, psychological
and spiritual needs to the forefront.

Loving yourself encourages partnership
rather than co-dependence...
allowing you both to remain whole, instead of fractions.

By loving yourself you give your partner and relationship
the best of you.

And when you are the best that you can be,
the relationship will thrive.

TRIGGERS SHOW YOU THE WOUNDS...

YOU NEVER KNEW YOU HAD

Most of us have some wounds hidden deep within us.

These wounds form as a result of pain and trauma
experienced through our life.

Most of these wounds are so deep,
we don't even know they're bleeding.

The more they bleed,
the likelier they are to get infected...
causing us to take actions in life that create
more wounds and more infections.

Feeling "triggered" is caused by having salt
rubbed into those wounds by a messenger.

Our first reaction is usually to go straight
for the messenger's jugular!

However, if we allow a few moments of self-awareness,
we'll start wondering where the fuck
those wounds came from in the first place.

Understanding where the wounds have come from,
& why they're still wide open,
empowers us to heal those wounds
and ensure they never open up and leave
us vulnerable to pain again.

So don't attack the messengers.
Thank them for you helping you heal.

DON'T BE A WET SPONGE

The answer to pretty much any problem
you can think of, is on the internet...

"How to lose weight, how to make money,
how to find love, how to be happy,
how to deal with pain & trauma..."

It's all there...
at the touch of a button.

Yet people are struggling now more than ever.

Not because they don't know what to do,
but because it's easier to consume information
than it is to take action and follow through.

We've become a society of wet sponges...
soaking up loads of information but doing fuck all with it.

Don't allow yourself to be a wet sponge.

Remember, twenty minutes of doing something
is more valuable than twenty hours
of thinking about doing something.

BEAUTY IS AN ILLUSION...

ENERGY IS REAL

How you feel about yourself
can and will make you appear...
10x more attractive or 10x less attractive

A person that loves who they are...
accepts themselves wholeheartedly...
& is in full flow with their purpose in life...

will exude a beautiful, radiant energy
that magnetises them from the core.

As a byproduct of the way this person
"feels" about themselves...
they'll naturally take care of their body & appearance,
whilst carrying themselves with a confident,
self-assured, yet humble attitude,
because they value and appreciate who they are.

This person will be perceived as being "attractive"
regardless of their outer shell.

You see, "beauty" and the way it's portrayed to us
via Instagram and the media... is an illusion.

The power be truly beautiful is always with you.

STOP CHASING HAPPINESS

"I'll be happy when it's the weekend"
"I'll be happy when I have more money"
"I'll be happy when I find love"
"I'll be happy when the kids grow up"
"I'll be happy when... blah blah blah"

No, you won't be happy.

You'll immediately fixate on the next "thing"
which'll leave you in a perpetual cycle
of chasing happiness and never catching it.

As a result, you could spend your whole life convinced
that happiness is just beyond your reach...
leaving you miserable.

Happiness ain't something you get
from the HR Department.
It's not conditional.
It's not something someone can hand to you.

It's a state of being that you choose to have.
It's a way of living. It's a way of thinking.

You can choose to be happy
in any given moment of your life.

"How the fuck I am supposed to do that!?"

By really, truly, deeply appreciating everything
you have in this present moment.

THIS IS WHAT YOU LOOK LIKE WHEN YOU BLAME YOURSELF

You've heard the famous Spiderman quote:
"With great power, comes great responsibility"

Well, here's an even more profound version:
"With great responsibility, comes great power"

Most people refuse to take responsibility for their
problems in life, because they believe that being
responsible is the equivalent to being at fault.

They are NOT the same thing.

Blaming = living in the past = no control

Self-blaming keeps you stuck in the past,
& will do nothing other than
perpetuate your fear, doubt and shame...
leaving you disempowered, helpless & victimised.

Responsibility = living in the now = full control

By taking full responsibility, your focus shifts
from the past to the present moment...
empowering you to change your circumstance.

So, stop beating yourself up...
no one cares whose fault it was, or who's to blame.

what matters, is how you're gonna go about
sorting your shit out.

SAVAGE QUESTIONS

Peeling back the layers

HOW WELL DO YOU ACTUALLY KNOW YOURSELF?

SAVAGE WISDOM

...And I don't mean your favourite food
or the type of music that gets you going.

I'm talkin' about the deepest, realest, rawest parts of you.
The parts hidden under multiple layers of ego, fear and denial.

Yeah, the real you.

Peeling back the layers and coming face to face with who you truly are,
will open your mind to an entirely new reality.

This "new reality" will allow you to...

think thoughts you've never thought,
feel feelings you've never felt,
& take actions you didn't even know were possible for you.

Being fully self-aware and 'at one' with who you are,
is the first step to really experiencing this life as your most empowered self.

Over the next few pages, you'll find a series of thought-provoking questions.

These questions, if you choose to allow them,
will take you on a beautifully deep journey of self-reflection...
where you'll come face to face with the real you.

Don't fight against, or resist, where your thoughts take you.
Let the questions run free in your mind.

Allow yourself to feel vulnerable,
and be savagely honest with your answers.

You may notice that more questions arise as you delve deeper.
That's good.
Answer those questions too & go with the flow of your own thoughts.

Some of the questions may make you feel uncomfortable.
That's good too.
It means you're peeling back layers that need to be peeled.

To really get the most out of this,
write your thoughts down as you think them.

Let your mind connect to your pen, and just free flow.

If you need more than the space provided,
use a separate piece of paper or journal.

If writing ain't your vibe, that's cool.
Sit back & let your mind drift as your thoughts peel back layer after layer.
Then, once you're done, simply jot your answer in a few words.

Spend at least 10-15 minutes on each question,
and aim to complete no more than four questions per day,
so that you can give all of your energy towards them.

Questions have power.
And by addressing deep questions to yourself,
you'll get profound answers from the person who knows you best... you.

Enjoy the journey...

How old would you be if you didn't know how old you were?

What's worse...
Failing or never trying?

When it's all said and done, will you have said more or done more – or vice versa?

Which person would be happier in life?
Person A) "Super good looking" with zero confidence & self-esteem.
Person B) "Unattractive" with high confidence & self-worth.

When was the last time you sat alone in complete silence?
With no tv, internet, music, or distractions whatsoever.

What's the difference between being alive and truly living?

Struggle is inevitable in life.
What are you willing to struggle for?

When you reminisce about this period of your life,
what will make you smile most?

If we learn & grow from our failures, then why is it so bad to fail?

What's one problem you're thankful you don't have right now?

Would the 10-year-old you, be proud of you?

What's on your "fuck-it" list?
(what you need to let go of, what you need to relax about, & what you need to say "fuck it!' to)

Which people in your life drain you the most?

How do you think people feel after engaging with you?

What are you not doing, that you know you should be doing?

What's worse...
Having your most treasured memories erased
or never being able to make new ones?

If challenge and adversity make you stronger, wiser, & more resilient...
What does an easy life make you?

What is your happiest childhood memory? What makes it so special?

What would you do differently if you knew nobody would judge?

**If you keep living the life you're living and doing the things you're doing…
How do you see your life pan out over the next 5 years?**

When was the last time you closed your eyes and paid attention to your breathing?

Who are the people that set your soul on fire and fill your heart with love?

**Would you rather have less work to do,
or be really busy with work you love doing?**

Is it possible to know the truth without challenging it first?

Should libraries put religious books in fiction or non-fiction?

What's the hardest, most brutal challenge you've overcome in your life?

At what time in your recent past have you felt most passionate and alive?

When was the last time you tried something new?

What's one mistake you'll never make again?

What has grown you the most as a person...
Your challenges and hardships or the comfortable yet enjoyable moments in life?

What does happiness truly mean to you?

When was the last time you laughed so hard it hurt?

Do you ask enough questions,
or are you happy to settle for what you already know?

Do we have free will or is everything predestined & already written in stone?

What are your most toxic/negative character traits?
(be fucking honest with yourself)

What is 'God'?

What does the best, most unfuckwithable version of you look like?
(how do they walk, talk, dress, behave & even smell)

What parts of your life don't reflect who you truly are
or who you're becoming?

Are you holding onto something you need to let go of?

What do you think about couples who throw soft, subtle digs at each other?

Are you healed or just trying not to think about it?

In your opinion, what does it mean to "make the most of life?"

What advice would the 80-year-old you give to the present you?

GO GET IT

It's yours

ADAM CAM

You can read all the self-help books.
You can listen to all the inspiring podcasts.
You can watch all the motivational videos.
And you can hire the best mentors, coaches & gurus.

All of those tools will only ever do one thing...

AMPLIFY WHAT IS ALREADY INSIDE YOU.

Deep down, beneath the insecurities, doubts, and fears...
you know exactly what you're capable of.

You even have moments where you get a glimpse
of your full potential...
and you fucking love it. Damn right you love it!
Because that's who you truly are.

If you take some time to fully absorb what's written
in this book,
you'll begin to feel that power amplify and flow through you.

Then you'll soon begin to realise that you're not broken,
you're not unworthy,
and you're not lacking in any way.

The only thing that has ever been wrong with you...
is the belief that there was ever anything wrong with you
in the first place.

So take this as your permission to show up in world as your truest, realest,
most authentic self.

Because you are enough,
just as you are.

Go get it Legend.

Peace, Love, Power,
Adam

Post pictures of your favourite images,
pages and quotes from the book using

#SavageWisdomBook

so I can find them, like them
and feature them on my page.

ABOUT THE AUTHOR

This is normally the part where I'm supposed to babble on about myself in third person.

Fuck that, let's keep it short, sweet and real.

I'm a Spiritual badass, who created a brand for Spiritual Badasses. Check it out at www.JustAura.com

You can also find me here:
Instagram: @adamcam10
TikTok: @adamcam10

Say hello at: Yep, that's a .CO not a .COM
adam@SavageWisdom.co

I would love to hear from you and get your thoughts and feedback on the book ☺

Made in the USA
Las Vegas, NV
06 November 2021